WHAT WOULD DRUCKER DO?

NURTURE GREAT ORGANIZATIONS AND SOCIETIES GUIDED BY PETER DRUCKER'S BEST QUOTES

EDITED BY
NIELS PFLAEGING

BETACODEX PRESS

Other books from BetaCodex Press:
- Organize for Complexity – Niels Pflaeging
- OpenSpace Beta – Silke Hermann/Niels Pflaeging
- Essays on Beta, Vol. 1 – Niels Pflaeging
- What Would Deming Do? – Niels Pflaeging (ed.)
- Cell Structure Design – Niels Pflaeging/Silke Hermann

© 2023 Niels Pflaeging, compilation rights only
BetaCodex Press – an imprint of qomenius GmbH
Matthias-Claudius-Strasse 16
D - 65185 Wiesbaden

Editor: Niels Pflaeging
Book design: Niels Pflaeging
Photos: Courtesy of the Drucker Institute
Fonts: League Gothic, Crete Round

ISBN Print 978-3-9484-7122-4
ISBN E-Book 978-3-9484-7123-1

For attractive volume discounts on BetaCodex Press books, which start at 10 copies, get in touch with contact@betacodexpress.com

Visit our website: betacodexpress.com
Check out our web shop at redforty2.com/shop

CONTENTS

About Drucker — 4

01 Society of Organizations — 6

02 The Knowledge Worker — 32

03 Work & Identity — 48

04 Performance & Purpose — 74

05 Decisions & Agreements — 104

06 Decentralize & Self-Organize — 116

08 Change & Transform — 136

07 Innovate & Renew — 150

09 Learn & Advance — 170

My Drucker — 180

Sources — 182

ABOUT DRUCKER

Peter F. Drucker (1909-2005) has been described as 'the greatest man in the history of management' and as 'the greatest management guru the world has yet seen. More modestly, Drucker himself quipped once he was 'just an old journalist'.

Born in Vienna, Drucker left Austria in 1927 to work in Hamburg and to study law. He began his professional life in Frankfurt as a financial reporter, and he never lost his journalistic eye for a witty aphorism or a cunning metaphor. Settling in America, in 1937, Drucker soon turned to teaching and consulting, and in 1946 produced his first management book, *The Concept of the Corporation*. His last article, *What Makes an Effective Executive* was published in 2004.

On occasion, Drucker described himself as a 'social ecologist.' He was a man of Renaissance breadth and depth well beyond the specialty that, arguably, he himself had created: *Management*. Drucker self-identified as a writer, first and foremost. As such, he was the most astute observer of modern organizational leadership and society of the 20th century. In the words of Charles Handy, the Drucker philosophy, or school of thinking, offers *"a view of organizations as if people mattered."* And: *"Peter Drucker lived so long, was so curious about so much, and covered so many topics in his writings that there is a deep well of thinking for the school to draw from."*

Drucker in his study, 1980s

In 1973, Peter Drucker wrote: "The citizen of today in every developed country is typically an employee. He works for one of the institutions. He looks to them for his livelihood. He looks to them for his opportunities. He looks to them for access to status and function in society, as well as for personal fulfillment and achievement. And: "The citizen of 1900 if employed worked for a small family-type operation; the small pop-and-mom store employing a helper or two; the family household; and so on. And of course, the great majority of people in those days, except in the most highly industrialized countries – such as Britain or Belgium – worked on the farm. Our society has become an employee society. In the early 1900s people asked, 'What do you do?' Today they tend to ask, 'Whom do you work for?'"

SOCIETY OF ORGANIZATIONS

Peter Drucker's Austrian passport, 1928

"An organization is not, like an animal, an end in itself, and successful by the mere act of perpetuating the species. An organization is an organ of society and fulfills itself by the contribution it makes to the outside environment."

TEE

"The society of organizations is new – only seventy years ago employees were a small minority in every society."

"Management is about human beings. The task of management is to make people capable of joint performance, to make their strengths effective and their weaknesses irrelevant. This is what organization is all about, and it is the reason that management is the critical, determining factor."

“Performing, responsible management is the alternative to tyranny and our only protection against it.”

"The purpose of an organization is to enable common men to do uncommon things."

"The 'non-profit' institution neither supplies goods or services nor
controls. Its 'product' is neither a
pair of shoes nor an effective reg-
ulation. Its product is a changed
human being. The non-profit institutions are human-change agents.
Their 'product' is a cured patient,
a child that learns, a young man
or woman grown into a self-
respecting adult; a changed
human life altogether."

"It is the purpose
of the organization,
and the grounds of
management authority,
to make human strength
productive."

"In every country there's
a cry for leadership. But it's the
wrong cry. When you have a mal-
function across the spectrum, you
don't have a people problem, you
have a systems problem. Modern
government needs innovation.
What we have now is roughly
400 years old. [...] It's time for new
thinking. The same holds true for
the economic theories that have
dominated the past 60 years or so.
Government - not businesses
or nonprofits - is going to be
the most important area of
entrepreneurship and innovation
over the next 25 years."

"Society, community, family
are all conserving institutions.
They try to maintain stability and
to prevent, or at least slow down,
change. But the organization
of the post-capitalist society of
organizations is a destabilizer.
Because its function is to put
knowledge to work – on tools,
processes, and products; on work;
on knowledge itself – it must
be organized for constant change.
It must be organized
for innovation."

"Free enterprise
cannot be justified as
being good for business.
It can be justified
only as being good
for society."

"No institution can possibly survive if it needs geniuses or supermen to manage it. It must be organized in such a way as to be able to get along under a leadership composed of average human beings."

"A business that does not show a profit at least equal to its cost of capital is irresponsible; it wastes society's resources. [...] Every organization must assume responsibility for its impact on employees, the environment, customers, and whomever and whatever it touches. That is social responsibility."

"The danger of total propaganda is not that propaganda will be believed. The danger is that nothing will be believed and that every communication becomes suspect. In the end, no communication is being received anymore. Everything anyone says is considered a demand and is resisted, resented, and in effect not heard at all. The end results of total propaganda are not fanatics, but cynics – but this, of course, may be even greater and more dangerous corruption."

"Freedom is not fun. It is not the same as individual happiness, nor is it security or peace or progress. It is a responsible choice. [...] It is not 'fun' but the heaviest burden laid on man to decide his own individual conduct as well as the conduct of society and to be responsible for both decisions."

"Insecurity – not economic but psychological insecurity – permeates the entire industrial situation. It creates fear; and since it is fear of the unknown and the unpredictable, it leads to a search for scapegoats and culprits. Only if we restore the worker's belief in the rationality and predictability of the forces that control his job, can we expect any policies in the industrial enterprise to be effective. In no other area can we hope to achieve so much so fast. All the basic forces – the objective requirements of society, the objective requirements of the enterprise, and the objective needs and requirements of the individual – work in the direction of making the industrial enterprise a functioning institution."

"Right conduct can never be established by procedure."

"It can be said
that there are no 'under-
developed countries.'
There are only
'undermanaged' ones."

"Capitalism as a social order and as a creed is the expression of the belief in economic progress as leading forward the freedom and equality of the individual in the free and equal society."

"Beware charisma. Charisma is 'hot' today. There is an enormous amount of talk about, and an enormous amount of books are written about the charismatic leader. But the desire for charisma is a political death wish."

"Management
always deals with
the nature of Man,
and with Good
and Evil."

"'It is not enough
for business to do well;
it must also do good.'
But in order to 'do good,'
a business must
first 'do well.'"

"The only things
that evolve by themselves
in an organization
are disorder, friction,
malperformance."

"Any organization
develops people.
It either forms them
or deforms them."

"For the social ecologist language is not 'communication.' It is not just 'message.' It is substance. It is the cement that holds humanity together. It creates community and communication. [...] Social ecologists need not be 'great' writers; but they have to be respectful writers, caring writers."

Drucker, in 1993: "The postwar [WWII] GI Bill of Rights – and the enthusiastic response to it on the part of America's veterans – signaled the shift to the knowledge society. Future historians may consider it the most important event of the twentieth century. We are clearly in the midst of this transformation; indeed, if history is any guide, it will not be completed until 2010 or 2020. But already it has changed the political, economic and moral landscape of the world." And: "By the end of this century knowledge workers will make up a third or more of the work force in the United States – as large a proportion as manufacturing workers ever made up, except in wartime. The majority of them will be paid at least as well as, or better than, manufacturing workers ever were. And the new jobs offer much greater opportunities."

THE KNOWLEDGE WORKER

Drucker, 1960s

"Knowledge workers cannot be satisfied with work that is only a livelihood."

"That knowledge
has become *the* resource,
rather than *a* resource,
is what makes our society
'post-capitalist.'"

"In a knowledge economy there are no such things as conscripts – there are only volunteers. The trouble is we have trained our managers to manage conscripts."

"Even if employed full-time
by the organization, fewer and
fewer people are 'subordinates' –
even in fairly low-level jobs.
Increasingly they are 'knowledge
workers.' And knowledge workers
are not subordinates; they are
'associates.' For, once beyond
the apprentice stage, knowledge
workers must know more about
their job than their boss does –
or else they are no good at all.
In fact, that they know more about
their job than anybody else in
the organization is part of the
definition of knowledge workers."

"This society in which
knowledge workers dominate is
in danger of a new 'class conflict'
between the large minority
of knowledge workers and the
majority of workers who will make
their livings through traditional
ways, either by manual work [...]
or by service work.
The productivity of knowledge
work – still abysmally low – will
predictably become the economic
challenge of the knowledge
society. On it will depend the
ability of the knowledge society
to give decent incomes,
and with them dignity and status,
to non-knowledge people."

"Knowledge is different from all other resources. It makes itself constantly obsolete, so that today's advanced knowledge is tomorrow's ignorance. And the knowledge that matters is subject to rapid and abrupt shifts."

"Knowledge work is not defined by quantity. Neither is knowledge work defined by its costs. Knowledge work is defined by its results. And for these, the size of the group and the magnitude of the managerial job are not even symptoms."

"The knowledge worker is not poverty-prone. He is in danger of alienation, to use the fashionable word for boredom, frustration, and silent despair."

"Knowledge without skill is unproductive. Knowledge does not eliminate skill. On the contrary, knowledge is fast becoming the foundation for skill. Only when knowledge is used as a foundation for skill does it become productive."

"Knowledge work is
specialized, and because
it is so specialized,
it is deeply splintered
in most organizations."

"Knowledge workers
are likely to outlive their
employing organization."

"Workers outliving organizations – and with it the need to be prepared for a second and different half of one's life – is a revolution for which practically no one is prepared. Nor is any existing institution, for example, the present retirement system."

"What to do with
the second half of one's life?
Knowledge workers are able
physically to keep on working
into old age, and well beyond any
traditional retirement age.
But they run a new risk: they may
become mentally finished.
What's commonly called
'burnout,' the most common
affliction of the fortysomething
knowledge worker, is very rarely
the result of stress. Its common,
all too common, cause is
boredom on the job."

"Employees may be our greatest liability, but people are our greatest opportunity."

Drucker, in 1973: "There is tremendous stress these days on liking people, helping people, getting along with people, as qualifications for a manager. These alone are never enough. In every successful organization there is one boss who does not like people, who does not help them, and who does not get along with them. Cold, unpleasant, demanding, he often teaches and develops more men than anyone else. He commands more respect than the most likable man ever could. He demands exacting workmanship of himself as well as of his men. He sets high standards and expects that they will be lived up to. He considers only what is right and never who is right. And though often himself a man of brilliance, he never rates intellectual brilliance above integrity in others. The manager who lacks these qualities of character – no matter how likable, helpful, or amiable, no matter even how competent or brilliant – is a menace and should be judged 'unfit to be a manager and a gentleman.'"

WORK
& IDENTITY

Drucker in the 1960s,
when the White House sought his wisdom

"Managing yourself
requires taking
responsibility
for relationships."

"By themselves, character and integrity do not accomplish anything. But their absence faults everything else. Here, therefore, is the one area where weakness is a disqualification by itself rather than a limitation on performance capacity and strength."

"We know very little about self-development. But we do know one thing: People in general, and knowledge workers in particular, grow according to the demands they make on them-selves. They grow according to what they consider to be achievement and attainment. If they demand little of themselves, they will remain stunted. If they demand a good deal of themselves, they will grow to giant stature – without any more effort than is expended by the non-achievers."

"Everyone must be ready to take over alone and without notice, and show himself saint or hero, villain or coward."

"The [career] stepladder is gone, and there's not even the implied structure of an industry's rope ladder. It's more like vines, and you bring your own machete. You don't know what you'll be doing next, or whether you'll work in a private office or one big amphitheater or even out of your home. You have to take responsibility for knowing yourself, so you can find the right jobs as you develop and as your family becomes a factor in your values and choices."

"Of all the important pieces of self-knowledge, understanding how you learn is the easiest to acquire."

"The fundamental reality for every worker, from sweeper to executive vice-president, is the eight hours or so that he spends on the job. In our society of organizations, it is the job through which the great majority has access to achievement, to fulfill-ment, and to community."

"That one can truly manage other people is by no means adequately proven. But one can always manage oneself."

"The danger is that executives
will become contemptuous
of information and stimulus that
cannot be reduced to computer
logic and computer language.
Executives may become blind to
everything that is perception
(i.e., event) rather than fact
(i.e., after the event).
The tremendous amount
of computer information may thus
shut out access to reality."

"The leaders who work most effectively, it seems to me, never say 'I.' And that's not because they have trained themselves not to say 'I.' They don't think 'I.' They think 'we'; they think 'team.' They understand their job to be to make the team function. They accept responsibility and don't sidestep it, but 'we' gets the credit. This is what creates trust, what enables you to get the task done."

"Psychological despotism,
whether enlightened or not,
is gross misuse of psychology.
The main purpose of psychology
is to acquire insight into, and
mastery of, oneself.
Not for nothing were what we
now call the behavioral sciences
originally called the moral sciences
and 'Know thyself' their main
precept. To use psychology to
control, dominate, and manipulate
others is self-destructive abuse
of knowledge. It is also
a particularly repugnant form
of tyranny."

"There is no such thing
as a 'good man.'
Good for what?
is the question."

"An employer has no business with a man's personality. Employment is a specific contract calling for a specific performance, and nothing else. Any attempt by an employer to go beyond this is usurpation. It is an immoral as well as illegal intrusion of privacy."

"The experience
of the human race
indicates strongly that
the only person in
abundant supply
is the universal
incompetent."

"Corporations once built to last like pyramids are now more like tents. Tomorrow they're gone or in turmoil. And this is true not only of companies in the headlines [...]. You can't design your life around a temporary organization."

"That people even in well paid jobs choose ever earlier retirement is a severe indictment of our organizations – not just business, but government service, the universities. These people don't find their jobs interesting."

"It is a law of nature that two moving bodies in contact with each other create friction. This is as true for human beings as it is for inanimate objects."

"Work, we know, is both
a burden and a need, both a curse
and a blessing. Unemployment
we long ago learned creates severe
psychological disturbances, not
because of economic deprivation,
but primarily because it under-
mines self-respect. Work is an
extension of personality.
It is achievement. It is one of
the ways in which a person defines
himself or herself, measures
his worth, and his humanity."

"The future will
not just happen
if one wishes
hard enough."

"To be information literate, you begin with learning what it is you need to know. Too much talk focuses on the technology, even worse on the speed of the gadget, always faster, faster. This kind of 'techie' fixation causes us to lose track of the fundamental nature of information in today's organization. To organize the way work is done, you have to begin with the specific job, then the information input, and finally the human relationships needed to get the job done."

"Knowledge technologists
are likely to become
the dominant social –
and perhaps also
political – force over
the next decades."

"The dominant factor in the next society will be something to which most people are only just beginning to pay attention: the rapid growth in the older population and the rapid shrinking of the younger generation. Politicians everywhere still promise to save the existing pensions system, but they – and their constituents – know perfectly well that in another 25 years people will have to keep working until their mid-70s, health permitting."

"Because the supply of young people will shrink, creating new employment patterns to attract and hold the growing number of older people (especially older educated people) will become increasingly important."

"Within 20 or 25 years, however, perhaps as many as half the people who work for an organization will not be employed by it, certainly not on a full-time basis. This will be especially true for older people. New ways of working with people at arm's length will increasingly become the central managerial issue of employing organizations, and not just of businesses."

Drucker, in 1973: "In an organization which manages by drives, people either neglect their job to get on with the current drive, or silently organize for collective sabotage of the drive in order to get their work done. In either event they become deaf to the cry of 'wolf.' And when the real crisis comes, when all hands should drop everything and pitch in, they treat it as just another case of management-created hysteria. Management by drive is a sure sign of confusion. It is an admission of incompetence. It is a sign that management does not think. But, above all, it is a sign that the company does not know what to expect of its managers and that, not knowing how to direct them, it misdirects them."

PERFORMANCE & PURPOSE

Drucker, 1970s

"If you want to know what a business is we have to start with its purpose, which must be found outside the business itself, [...] in society, in fact, since a business enterprise is an organ of society. There is only one valid definition of business purpose – namely to create a customer."

"A time of turbulence
is a dangerous time,
but its greatest danger
is a temptation
to deny reality."

"Efficiency is concerned with doing things right. Effectiveness is doing the right things."

"Management
by objectives works if
you know the objectives.
Ninety percent
of the time you don't."

"Profit is not the explanation, cause, or rationale of business behavior and business decisions, but rather the test of their validity. If archangels instead of businessmen sat in directors' chairs, they would still have to be concerned with profitability, despite their total lack of personal interest in making profits."

"Profit is the ultimate test of business performance."

"If you think training
is expensive,
try ignorance."

"People in any organization are always attached
to the obsolete –
the things that should
have worked but did not,
the things that once
were productive
and no longer are."

"No financial manager ever understood the business. Because financial people believe that companies make money. But companies make shoes. The money is at the end, not at the beginning. For financial managers, that's dreadfully hard to understand."

"A well-managed plant,
I soon learned, is a quiet place.
A factory that is 'dramatic,'
a factory in which the 'epic of
industry' is unfolded before the
visitor's eyes, is poorly managed.
A well-managed factory is boring.
Nothing exciting happens in it because the crises have been
anticipated and have been
converted into routine."

"Control has to be
by feedback from the
work done. The work
itself has to provide
the information.
If it has to be checked
all the time, there
is no control."

"Work is a process,
and any process needs
to be controlled.
To make work productive,
therefore, requires
building the appropriate
controls into the
process of work."

"But above all, meetings have to be the exception rather than the rule. An organization in which everybody meets all the time is an organization in which no one gets anything done."

"The oft-repeated quip, 'I'm sorry to write you a long letter, as I did not have time to write a short one,' could be applied to meetings: 'I'm sorry to imprison you in this long meeting, as I did not have time to prepare a short one.'"

"The man who focuses on
efforts and who stresses
his downward authority is
a subordinate no matter how
exalted his title and rank.
But the man who focuses on
contribution and who takes
responsibility for results,
no matter how junior, is in the
most literal sense of the phrase,
'top management.' He holds
himself accountable for the
performance of the whole."

"Those who perform
love what they are doing."

"Absolute size by itself
is no indicator of success
and achievement,
let alone of managerial
competence.
Being the right size is."

"The idea that growth is by itself a goal is altogether a delusion. There is no virtue in a company's getting bigger. The right goal is to become better. Growth, to be sound, should be the result of doing the right things. By itself, growth is vanity and little else."

"Growth as a goal,
to repeat, is delusion.
William James, the
American philosopher,
talked of the 'bitch
goddess success.'
A philosopher of
business today might
well talk of the
'bitch goddess growth.'"

William James (1842 – 1910) was an American philosopher, historian, and psychologist, and the first educator to offer a psychology course in the United States.

"Nonprofits need more not less management, precisely because they don't have a financial bottom line. Both their mission and their 'product' have to be clearly defined and continually assessed. And most have to learn how to attract and hold volunteers whose satisfaction is measured in responsibility and accomplishment, not wages."

"The only profit center
of a business is
a customer whose
check hasn't bounced."

"All of us [Juran, Deming and I] knew that quality doesn't cost. And that the accounting model is a smear and a delusion: Because it hides the cost of not doing. Which is 70%. [...] Doing things is cheap. Not doing things is expensive. Cost accounting does not measure these things."

W. Edwards Deming (1900–1993) and Joseph M. Juran (1904–2008) were pioneers of the quality movement and – working independently from each other – hugely influential in post-WWII Japan. Both are well-known for their theories of management.

"One cannot hire a hand – the whole man always comes with it."

"The best plan is only good intentions unless it *degenerates into work.*"

"The preference should be
for simple compensation systems
rather than for complex ones.
It should be for compensation systems that allow judgment
to be used and that enable pay to
be fitted to the job of the individual
rather than impose one formula on
everybody. All one can do is
to watch lest the compensation
system reward the wrong
behavior, emphasize the wrong
results, and direct people away
from performance for
the common good."

"J. P. Morgan, who certainly cannot be accused of not liking money, gave an order to his investment people never to invest in a company in which a CEO earned more than 30 percent more than the next layer. That CEO, he said, can't build a team, and the company is mismanaged.
He also once said that the proper ratio for salaries for employed people, between the top people and the rank and file should be twenty-fold, post-tax. That's the highest. Beyond that, you create social tension."

J. P. Morgan (1837 – 1913) was an American financier and investment banker who dominated corporate finance on Wall Street throughout the Gilded Age.

"Stock option plans reward the executive for doing the wrong thing. Instead of asking, 'Are we making the right decision?' he asks, 'How did we close today?' It is encouragement to loot the corporation."

"I believe it is socially and morally unforgivable when managers reap huge profits for themselves but fire workers."

In 1973, Peter Drucker wrote: "The work relationship has to be based on mutual respect. Psychological despotism is basically contemptuous—far more contemptuous than the traditional *Theory X*. It does not assume that people are lazy and resist work, but it assumes that the manager is healthy while everybody else is sick. It assumes that the manager is strong while everybody else is weak. It assumes that the manager knows while everybody else is ignorant. It assumes that the manager is right, whereas everybody else is stupid. These are the assumptions of foolish arrogance."

DECISIONS
& AGREEMENTS

Drucker, 1970s

"'Gentlemen, I take it we are all in complete agreement on the decision here.' Everyone around the table nodded assent. 'Then,' continued Mr. Sloan, 'I propose we postpone further discussion of this matter until our next meeting to give ourselves time to develop disagreement and perhaps gain some understanding of what the decision is all about.'"

Alfred P. Sloan (1875 – 1966) was an American business executive in the automotive industry. He was a long-time president, chairman and CEO of General Motors Corporation.

"The first rule in decision-making is that one does not make a decision unless there is disagreement."

"A decision
without an alternative
is a desperate
gambler's throw."

"A decision is
a judgment. It is a choice
between alternatives.
It is rarely a choice
between right and wrong.
It is at best a choice
between 'almost right'
and 'probably wrong' –
but much more often
a choice between two
courses of action neither
of which is probably
more nearly right
than the other."

"Decision-making is a time machine that synchronizes into a single time – the present – a great number of divergent time spans."

"Anyone who knows Western businesses, government agencies, or educational institutions knows that their managers make far too many small decisions as a rule. And nothing causes as much trouble in an organization as a lot of small decisions."

"Authority without responsibility is illegitimate; but so is responsibility without authority."

AB

"If you wait until you have made the decision and then start to 'sell' it, it's unlikely to ever become effective."

"The right answer
to the wrong problem
is very difficult to fix."

"The one man to distrust,
however, is the man
who never makes
a mistake, never commits
a blunder, never fails
in what he tries to do.
He is either a phony,
or he stays with the safe,
the tried, and the trivial."

In 1954, Drucker wrote: "Self-control means stronger motivation: a desire to do the best, rather than just enough to get by." In 1973, he added: "Of all design principles available so far, federal decentralization comes closest to satisfying all design specifications. It also has the widest scope. Both operating work and innovative work can be organized as decentralized autonomous businesses. [...] Federal decentralization of the business, if done properly, makes for strong and effective top managements. It frees top management for the top-management tasks."

DECENTRALIZE & SELF-ORGANIZE

Drucker, 1980s

"The model for management that we have right now is the opera. The conductor of an opera has a very large number of different groups that he has to pull together. The soloists, the chorus, the ballet, the orchestra, all have to come together – but they have a common score. What we are increasingly talking about today are diversified groups that have to write the score while they perform. What you need now is a good jazz group. And if you want to have a really good jazz group, how large can it be? How large can it be when you have people who improvise on their own and the group realizes that the trumpet player is now playing his solo and everybody needs to stop and support him? You can use seven to nine people – maximum. If you get more, you have to score."

"Self-control means
stronger motivation:
a desire to do the best
rather than just
enough to get by."

"I do not use the buzzword participative. Worse yet is the empowerment concept. It is not a great step forward to take power out at the top and put it in at the bottom. It's still power. To build achieving organizations, you must replace power with responsibility."

"I'm not comfortable with
the word manager anymore,
because it implies subordinates.
I find myself using executive more,
because it implies responsibility
for an area, not necessarily
dominion over people. [...]
The new organizations need to go
beyond senior/junior polarities
to a blend with sponsor and
mentor relations. In the traditional
organization – the organization
of the last 100 years – the skeleton,
or internal structure, was
a combination of rank and power.
In the emerging organization,
it has to be mutual understanding
and responsibility."

"Management textbooks still talk mainly about managing subordinates. But you no longer evaluate an executive in terms of how many people report to him or her. That standard doesn't mean as much as the complexity of the job, the information it uses and generates, and the different kinds of relationships needed to do the work."

"Measuring requires, first and foremost, analytical ability. But it also demands that measurement be used to make self-control possible rather than abused to control people from the outside and above—that is, to dominate them. It is the common violation of this principle that largely explains why measurement is the weakest area in the work of the manager today. As long as measurements are abused as a tool of control (for instance, as when measurements are used, as a weapon of an internal secret police that supplies audits and critical appraisals of a manager's performance to the boss without even sending a carbon copy to the manager himself) measuring will remain the weakest area in the manager's performance."

"An excess of meetings indicates that jobs have not been defined clearly, have not been structured big enough, have not been made truly responsible. Also the need for meetings indicates that the decisions and relations analyses either have not been made at all or have not been applied. The rule should be to minimize the need for people to get together to accomplish anything."

"There is a point
of complexity beyond
which a business is
no longer manageable."

"It does not matter whether the worker wants responsibility or not, [...] The enterprise must demand it of him."

"Teams fail – and the failure rate has been high – primarily because they do not impose on themselves the self-discipline and responsibility that are required precisely because of the high degree of freedom team organization gives. No task force can be 'permissive' and function. This is the reason why the same young educated people who clamor for team work tend so often in reality to resist it. It makes tremendous demands on self-discipline."

"What has changed manufacturing and sharply pushed up productivity, are new concepts, such as 'lean manufacturing.' Information and automation are less important than new theories of manufacturing, which are an advance comparable to the arrival of mass production [in the 1920s]."

"Traditional organizations rest on command authority. Information-based organizations rest on responsibility."

"In attracting and holding
knowledge workers,
we already know what
does not work: bribery."

"Autonomous managers in a federal structure cannot be content with 'reports.' They must think through what top management needs to understand. And they must accept the responsibility for educating their top management."

"Federal decentralization has great clarity and considerable economy. It makes it easy for each member of the autonomous business to understand his own task and to understand the task of the whole business. It has high stability and is yet adaptable."

"Decentralization must not create a weak center. On the contrary, one of the main purposes of federal organization is to strengthen top management and to make it capable of doing its own work rather than be forced to supervise, coordinate, and prop up operating work. Federal decentralization will work only if the top-management job is clearly defined and thought through."

"Federal decentralization requires centralized controls and common measurements. Whenever a federal organization gets into trouble, the reason is always that the measurements at the disposal of the center are not good enough. As a result, personal supervision has to be substituted. Both the managers of the autonomous businesses and top management must know what is expected of each business, what is meant by 'performance,' and what developments are important. To give autonomy, one must have confidence. And this requires controls that make opinions unnecessary."

"The multinationals of 2025 are likely to be held together and controlled by strategy. There will still be ownership, of course. But alliances, joint ventures, minority stakes, know-how agreements and contracts will increasingly be the building blocks of a confederation. This kind of organization will need a new kind of top management."

Drucker, in 2004: "I consider myself a 'social ecologist,' concerned with man's man-made environment the way the natural ecologist studies the biological environment. [...] The discipline itself boasts an old and distinguished lineage. Its greatest document is *Alexis de Tocqueville's Democracy in America*. But no one is as close to me in temperament, concepts, and approach as the mid-Victorian Englishman *Walter Bagehot*. Living (as I have) in an age of great social change, Bagehot first saw the emergence of new institutions: civil service and cabinet government, as cores of a functioning democracy, and banking as the center of a functioning economy. A 100 years after Bagehot, I was first to identify management as the new social institution of the emerging society of organizations and, a little later, to spot the emergence of knowledge as the new central resource, and knowl-

edge workers as the new ruling class of a society that is not only 'postindustrial' but post-socialist and, increasingly, post-capitalist. As it had been for Bagehot, for me too the tension between the need for continuity and the need for innovation and change was central to society and civilization."

CHANGE
& TRANSFORM

Drucker, 1990s

"Effective leadership –
and again this is very
old wisdom – is not based
on being clever;
it is based primarily on
being consistent."

"Culture – no matter
how defined –
is singularly persistent."

"The moment people talk of 'implementing' instead of 'doing,' and of 'finalizing' instead of 'finishing,' the organization is already running a fever."

"The most effective way to manage change successfully is to create it."

"Today's certainties
always become
tomorrow's absurdities."

"A change is something
people do,
a fad is something
people talk about."

"This defines
entrepreneur and
entrepreneurship –
the entrepreneur always
searches for change,
responds to it,
and exploits it as
an opportunity."

"Without systematic and purposeful abandonment, an organization will be overtaken by events."

"Organizations have a gravity. Their weight is constantly being pushed into being program focused and mediocrity focused. One has to fight it all the time. There's another subtle problem. The typical kind of daily problem can be fixed very fast. To build from first-class performance to excellence takes a long time; then you see tremendous results."

"Today's businesses, especially
American businesses, are
upsetting people unnecessarily.
Not because there is too much
change, but because they do
not even try to emphasize
the continuity, the relationships,
the mutual responsibilities,
which convert the mob into
an organization. [...] But when
you introduce change, it's very
important to maintain continuity
and the commitment to fundamental values, which don't change. [...]
On that basis, you can have
very rapid change and
it doesn't upset people."

"Too many managers still go by averages. They still talk about 'our engineers.' And I say, 'Brother, you don't have engineers. You have Joe and Mary and Jim and Bob, and each is different.' You can no longer manage a work force. You manage individuals."

"To survive and succeed,
every organization
will have to turn itself into
a change agent."

In 1985, Drucker wrote: "The literature is full of discussions of these questions; full of stories of the 'entrepreneurial personality' and of people who will never do anything but innovate. In the light of our experience – and it is considerable – these discussions are pointless. By and large, people who do not feel comfortable as innovators or as entrepreneurs will not volunteer for such jobs; the gross misfits eliminate themselves. The others can learn the practice of innovation."

INNOVATE & RENEW

Drucker, 1990s

"The people who work within these industries or public services know that there are basic flaws. But they are almost forced to ignore them and to concentrate instead on patching here, improving there, fighting the fire or caulking that crack. They are thus unable to take the innovation seriously, let alone to try to compete with it. They do not, as a rule, even notice it until it has grown so big as to encroach on their industry or service, by which time it has become irreversible. In the meantime, the innovators have the field to themselves."

"Many brilliant people believe that ideas move mountains.
But bulldozers move mountains; ideas show where the bulldozers should go to work."

"Ideas are somewhat
like babies – they are born
small, immature, and shapeless.
They are promise rather than
fulfillment. In the innovative
company, executives do not say,
'This is a damn-fool idea.'
Instead they ask, 'What would
be needed to make this embryonic,
half-baked, foolish idea into
something that makes sense,
that is an opportunity for us?'"

"The brilliant insight
is not by itself
achievement."

"I don't care for the popular theory that a generation of entrepreneurs can solve our problems. Entrepreneurs are monomaniacs. Managers are synthesizers who bring resources together and have that ability to 'smell' opportunity and timing. [...] You need the invaluable listener who says, 'I hear us all trying to kill the new product to protect the old one.'"

"Innovation is
the specific tool of
entrepreneurs, the means
by which they exploit
change as an opportunity
for a different business
or a different service."

"Any existing organization, whether a business, a church, a labor union, or a hospital, goes down fast if it does not innovate. Conversely, any new organization, whether a business, a church, a labor union, or a hospital, collapses if it does not manage. Not to innovate is the single largest reason for the decline of existing organizations. Not to know how to manage is the single largest reason for the failure of new ventures."

"Even today
few businessmen
understand that research,
to be productive, has
to be the 'disorganizer,'
the creator of a different
future and the enemy of
today. In most industrial
laboratories, 'defensive
research' aimed at
perpetuating today,
predominates."

"There is only
one definition
of ‘entrepreneur‘.
An entrepreneur
is someone who gets
something new done."

"The first one certainly has the pioneer's advantage. But may I respectfully point out that there has been no case in history where the pioneer became the dominant producer, whether you are talking about a business or a science. The most successful innovators are the creative imitators, the Number Two."

"Innovative ideas are like frogs' eggs: of a thousand hatched, only one or two survive to maturity."

"Innovation requires us to systematically identify changes that have already occurred in a business – in demographics, in values, in technology or science – and then to look at them as opportunities. It also requires something that is most difficult for existing companies to do: to abandon rather than defend yesterday."

"Without systematic and purposeful abandonment, an organization will be overtaken by events. It will squander its best resources on things it should never have been doing or should no longer do."

"The majority of successful new inventions or products don't succeed in the market for which they were originally designed. Many businesses disappear because the founder-entrepreneur insists that he or she knows better than the market. He or she rejects success."

"When the business grows, the person who founded it is incredibly busy. Rapid growth puts an enormous strain on a business. You outgrow your production facilities. You outgrow your management capabilities."

"There were no large corporations when the railroad in this country became one. And there was no competition. The railroad didn't displace anybody, didn't cause any dislocation. But now the world is full of organizations. And we're in turmoil because so many of the organizations whose roots go back 100 years or more are not going to survive. The large organization has to learn to innovate, or it won't survive."

"The theory of the business must be known and understood throughout the organization. That is easy in an organization's early days. But as it becomes successful, an organization tends increasingly to take its theory for granted, becoming less and less conscious of it. Then the organization becomes sloppy. It begins to cut corners. It begins to pursue what is expedient rather than what is right. It stops thinking. It stops questioning. It remembers the answers but has forgotten the questions. The theory of the business becomes 'culture.' But culture is no substitute for discipline, and the theory of the business is a discipline."

"The need to organize for change also requires a high degree of decentralization. That is because the organization must be structured to make decisions quickly. And those decisions must be based on closeness – to performance, to the market, to technology, and to all the many changes in society, the environment, demographics, and knowledge that provide opportunities for innovation if they are seen and utilized."

Drucker, in 2004: "The upward mobility of the knowledge society comes at a high price: the psychological pressures and emotional traumas of the rat race.
There can be winners only if there are losers. This was
not true of earlier societies." And: "Japanese young-
sters suffer sleep deprivation because they spend
their evenings at a crammer to help them pass their
exams. Otherwise they will not get into the pres-
tige university of their choice, and thus into a good
job. Other countries, such as America, Britain, and
France, are also allowing their schools to become
viciously competitive. That this has happened over
such a short time – no more than 30 or 40 years – indicates how much the fear of failure has already per-
meated the knowledge society. Given this competitive struggle, a growing number of highly successful
knowledge workers – business man-
agers, university teachers, museum
directors, doctors – 'plateau' in
their forties. If their work is all
they have, they are in trouble.
Knowledge workers therefore
need to develop some serious outside interest."

LEARN
& ADVANCE

Drucker, 1990s

"As a rule, theory does not precede practice. Its role is to structure and codify already proven practice. Its role is to convert the isolated and 'atypical' from exception to 'rule' and 'system,' and therefore into something that can be learned and taught and, above all, into something that can be generally applied."

"Redesigning a job and then teaching the worker the new way to do it, which is what Taylor did and taught, cannot by itself sustain ongoing learning. Training is only the beginning of learning. Indeed, as the Japanese can teach us (thanks to their ancient tradition of Zen), the greatest benefit of training comes not from learning something new but from doing better what we already do well."

Frederick W. Taylor (1856 – 1915) was an American engineer and inventor. He was the creator of the Scientific Management approach, which today is often referred to as Taylorism.

"Thirty years from now the big university campuses will be relics. Universities won't survive. It's as large a change as when we first got the printed book. Do you realize that the cost of higher education has risen as fast as the cost of health care? And for the middle-class family, college education for their children is as much of a necessity as is medical care – without it the kids have no future. Such totally uncontrollable expenditures, without any visible improvement in either the content or the quality of education, means that the system is rapidly becoming untenable. Higher education is in deep crisis."

"Education gives you
neither experience
nor wisdom."

"Skills one can acquire. Values no."

"No one learns as much about a subject as one who is forced to teach it."

"People, especially the young, think that they want all the freedom they can get, but it is very demanding, very difficult to think through who you are and what you do best."

"I think the growth industry of the future in this country and the world will soon be the continuing education of adults. [...] I think the educated person of the future is somebody who realizes the need to continue to learn. That is the new definition and it is going to change the world we live in and work in."

MY DRUCKER

Peter Drucker's body of work is so vast – spanning seven decades, almost 40 books and 1.500 articles – that making the necessary choices on topics and specific quotes to appear in this compilation has been something of a challenge during the editing of this volume. Once I started thinking about this book, I soon noticed that by now, almost two decades after the master's death, the lion's share of 'Drucker quotes' found on the web is wrongly attributed: They are not actually Drucker's! A case in point is the now ubiquitous *Culture eats strategy for breakfast* quip, which is usually attributed to Drucker, but clearly not his. Checking the veracity of the most widely circulated quotes attributed to Drucker has been a bit of detective work. This book of quotes is trying to set the record straight: Included in this volume you will only find quotes that I was able to trace back to Drucker himself. You will find that there is no shortage of crisp, contemporary, even timeless insight.

Drucker has been a unique figure in business and management theory and writing, as he covered a remarkable range of topics. I have attempted to focus this volume on just nine topics. Other important themes in Drucker's writing, like *non-profit organizations*, *government*, *marketing*, or *ethics of business*, would have been obvious choices – but these themes may be the topic for yet another book of quotes.

One thing I most appreciate in Drucker was his unceasing ability and willingness to informed dissent. He was indeed a master of the insightful objection. Drucker was quite happy with facing the consequences of being a relentless contrarian. "I have always been a loner," Drucker said once. "I work best outside. That's where I'm most effective. I would be a very poor manager. Hopeless. And a company job would bore me to death. I enjoy being an outsider."

While Drucker is often lauded for his predictions of trends, he sought to clarify his stance on prediction, in a 1996 interview: "I don't speculate about the future. It's not given to mortals to see the future. All one can do is analyze the present, especially those parts that do not fit what everybody knows and takes for granted. Then one can apply to this analysis the lessons of history and come out with a few possible scenarios. Then one comes out with a few probabilities. Even then there are always surprises."

This book is an invitation to turn to Drucker's original work and devour his classics. The master had witty things to say about his own oeuvre, too, of course. Such as this: "There are many books I could have written that are better than the ones I actually wrote. My best book would have been 'Managing Ignorance', and I'm very sorry I didn't write it."

Drucker by the pool, 1989

SOURCES

The source of each quote is indicated at the bottom of the quote's page – see title abbreviations below.

Quoted books by Peter F. Drucker:

1939: The End of Economic Man (EEM)

1946: Concept of the Corporation (CC)

1954: The Practice of Management (TPoM)

1959: Landmarks of Tomorrow (LoT)

1967: The Effective Executive (TEE)

1969: The Age of Discontinuity (AoD)

1970: Technology, Management and Society (TMS)

1973: Management: Tasks, Responsibilities, Practices (MTRP)

1978: Adventures of a Bystander (AB)

1985: Innovation and Entrepreneurship: Practice and Principles (IEPP)

1986: The Frontiers of Management (FoM)

1993: The New Realities (TNR)

1990: Managing the Non-Profit Organization (MNPO)

1993: Post-Capitalist Society (PCS)

1993: The Ecological Vision (TEV)

1995: Managing in a Time of Great Change (MTGC)

SOURCES

... continued

1998: Peter Drucker on the Profession of Management (PDPM)

1999: Managing Oneself (MO)

1999: Management Challenges for the 21st Century (MC21)

2001: The Essential Drucker (TED)

2002: Managing in the Next Society (MNS)

2004: The Daily Drucker – with Maciariello, J. A. (TDD)

2008: Management, Revised Edition (MRE)

2017: The Peter F. Drucker Reader (PDR)

Other quoted sources:

1993: HBR interview (HBR)

1996: WIRED interview (WIR)

1996: INC. interview (INC)

1996: Leader to Leader interview (LtL)

2001: The Next Society - Economist article (ECO)

2001: Leading in a Time of Change (LTC)

2023: Drucker Institute website (DI)

Additional quotes as indicated

Photos in this volume courtesy of the
Drucker Institute, drucker.institute

OTHER BOOKS

... from BetaCodex Press

Essays on Beta, Vol. 1
Niels Pflaeging.
1st ed.

OpenSpace Beta
Silke Hermann and
Niels Pflaeging. 3rd ed.

Organize for Complexity
Niels Pflaeging.
6th ed.

What Would Deming Do?
Niels Pflaeging (editor).
1st ed.

Available from your favorite book store –
and also from redforty2.com/shop